# Senior Living With Dick and Jane

**Written by Roseann Hotz Woodka, PhD**

Illustrated by Elena Bogatireva

*Senior Living with Dick and Jane* is the final book of three. It is preceded by *Precious Moments with Dick and Jane* and *Double Trouble with Dick and Jane*. Together the books chronicle the life story of rescued puppies who became therapy dogs, loved by everyone.

No longer puppies and "dogettes," they are now senior dogs who still get into mischief. As the book progresses, Dick and Jane's health declines. They don't hear as well, see as well, or have as much energy as they had in the first two books.

*Senior Living with Dick and Jane* follows the same format as *Precious Moments* and *Double Trouble*. It is divided into nine sections: "Seniors," "Helping Mommy," "Yoga," "Health," "Grandma," "Saying Goodbye," "Christmas," "One Year Later," and "Healing."

As with the prior books, *Senior Living with Dick and Jane* is designed to be read straight through, or it can be started and stopped according to the interest of the reader and the listener. The series can be read in sequence to get the full story of Dick and Jane's life. As you will see, the storyteller shifts between the characters of Dick and Jane depending on the focus of the vignette.

There is very little written for children about the loss of a pet. It is my hope that *Senior Living with Dick and Jane* can help parents and children understand and accept that sadness and tears are a healthy part of the grieving process.

Laughing at the antics is also a part of healing. The memories are ours to keep. Giving and receiving love never ends.

I feel so glad to be able to share Dick and Jane's story with you.

*Roseann*

*Tired after meeting the staff at PFC*

## TRIBUTE

In honor of Dr. Kathleen Neuhoff and the staff at Magrane Pet Medical Center, Mishawaka, IN, who loved, laughed and cared for Dick and Jane throughout the later years of their lives. They supported me and cried with me as I had to say "Goodbye" to my beloved, furry, four-legged children.

An additional tribute to Dr. Thomas McNeill who shared my joy at the very beginning of Dick and Jane's entry into my life. His kindness and compassion set the stage for all three of us to enjoy going to the doggie doctor.

"the last chapter..."

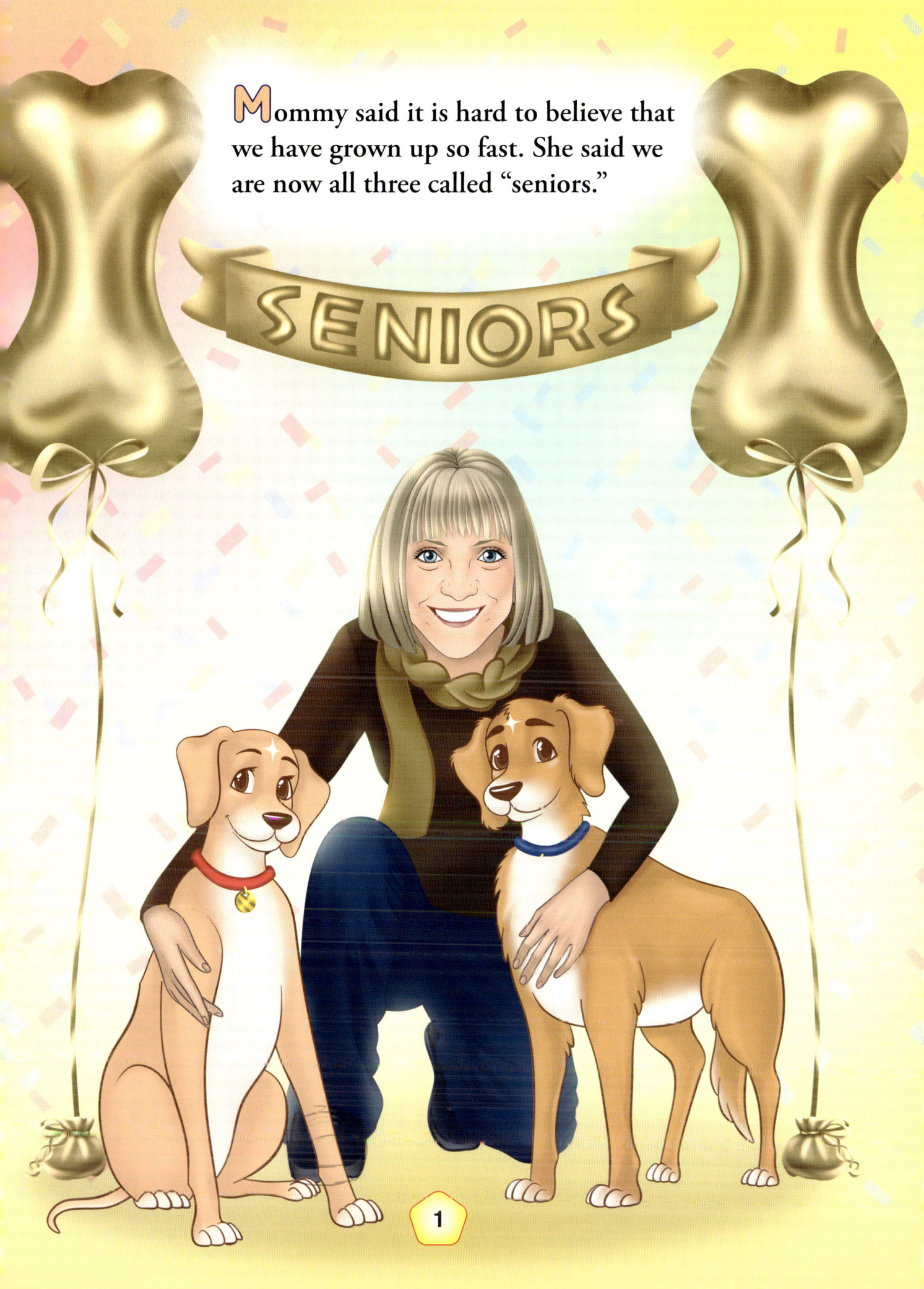

Mommy said it is hard to believe that we have grown up so fast. She said we are now all three called "seniors."

Being a senior doesn't mean that we can't get into mischief and have fun, though. Even Mommy has fun and can be really silly.

We still like to swim with our magic ball. We use lifejackets now since our legs aren't as strong as they used to be. One life jacket is bright yellow and the other is bright red. We love having our own special colors.

# Helping Mommy

Mommy puts tennis balls in the dryer. She said the tennis balls make her clothes soft and fluffy. One time when Mommy turned her back, we jumped in the dryer and each got our own tennis ball. We thought we would be soft and fluffy, too, but it didn't work.

To wash the dishes, we take turns like human brothers and sisters. Dick licks the plates and Jane uses the dish brush. When they are all clean, Jane dries the plates with the dish towel that she wears around her neck. We think our way is better than using the dishwasher! (Mommy ends up washing them, anyway).

Mommy has a really little car. On nice days she puts the top down. We love to ride in it and hang our heads out of the window. Our ears blow in the wind. It feels so good.

Sometimes other drivers whistle at us. Mommy says it's because the car is so cute. But we think it's because WE are so cute.

One day Mommy went to the grocery store but she forgot to put the top up. (That was a big mistake). It didn't take us long to figure out that we could go shopping with Mommy and help her pick out our favorite treats. All we had to do was jump out of the car…and so we did!

The most amazing thing happened when we got to the door. It opened magically just for us. We ran down the aisles looking for Mommy. The grocery store people chased us. We love to play "catch us if you can." We wonder if the store people had as much fun as we did. As for Mommy…she pretended she didn't know us.

# Yoga Class

Sometimes we get to go to Mommy's yoga class. She said yoga helps her relax. We like to do the "down dog" pose. We try to help the people do it right. We must be good teachers…they do it almost as good as we do!

When the people lay down at the end of the class, we roll around and give them kisses. They giggle so we give them more kisses. We think they like it.

# Health

Mommy doesn't see little letters as well as she used to. Sometimes she wears glasses. We put Mommy's glasses on so we can read just like she does. Her books aren't all that interesting except the ones about us, of course. We like to look at books and see pictures of us when we were little. We were really tiny and REALLY cute.

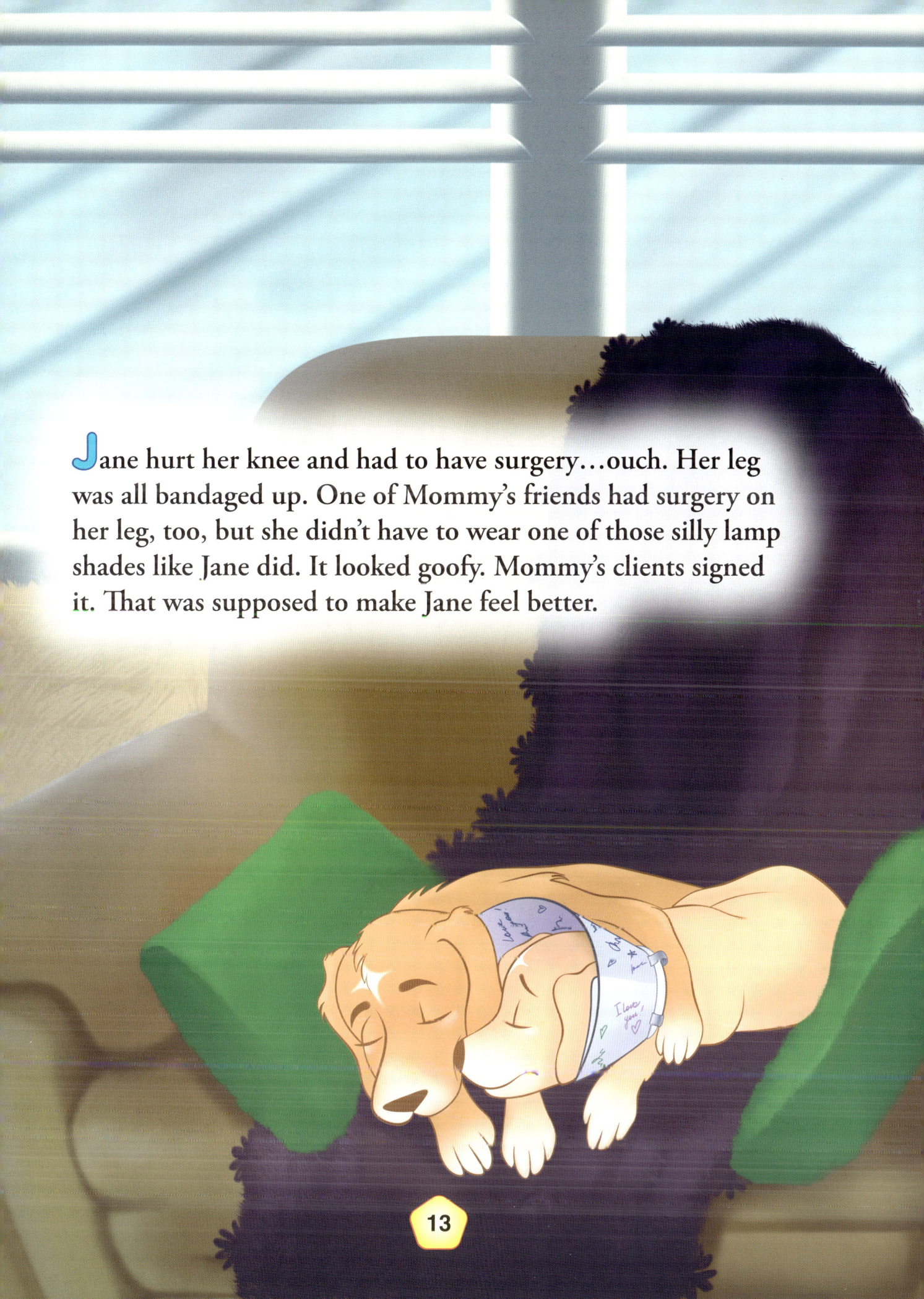

Jane hurt her knee and had to have surgery…ouch. Her leg was all bandaged up. One of Mommy's friends had surgery on her leg, too, but she didn't have to wear one of those silly lamp shades like Jane did. It looked goofy. Mommy's clients signed it. That was supposed to make Jane feel better.

Dick got a bad infection on his tummy. The doctor said it wouldn't heal if he kept scratching it. This time it was Dick who had to wear the silly lamp shade. He wasn't very happy about it.

Mommy said older people and older dogs, like Jane, sometimes get this thing called arthritis which hurts. She got a special kind of treatment with a bright light. She had to wear funny looking goggles to protect her eyes. The doctor, Mommy and I had to wear them, too. We couldn't tell which one of us looked silliest.

We were told that we weren't hearing as well as we used to. Sometimes we just don't WANT to hear. Somebody said it is called selective hearing. That means we only hear what we want to hear…treat, ball and swim. Some people have selective hearing, too, and they have to wear hearing aids. We are glad they don't have hearing aids for dogs.

**M**ommy said when people get older, they don't have as much energy as they did when they were young. That must happen to dogs, too. We were sleeping more and getting into mischief less.

# Grandma

We really loved our mommy's mommy. That would be our grandma. She played with us, rubbed our tummies, and gave us treats. She thought we were funny even when we played "florist" with her violets on her living room floor. We thought the flowers looked very pretty.

When Grandma got old and confused, she went to live with some other people who were old and confused. Mommy took us to visit Grandma and her friends. They laughed at us and gave us treats. It was a good deal!

Some days Grandma did not know who Mommy was, but she always knew who we were…her favorite furry, four-legged grandchildren. She even had two stuffed puppies that she named Dick and Jane. We knew we were really special. She loved us and we loved her.

When we woke up one morning, Mommy said we wouldn't get to visit Grandma anymore. She said Grandma went to heaven. We were so sad. Mommy hugged us really tight. We cried doggie tears, and Mommy cried Mommy tears.

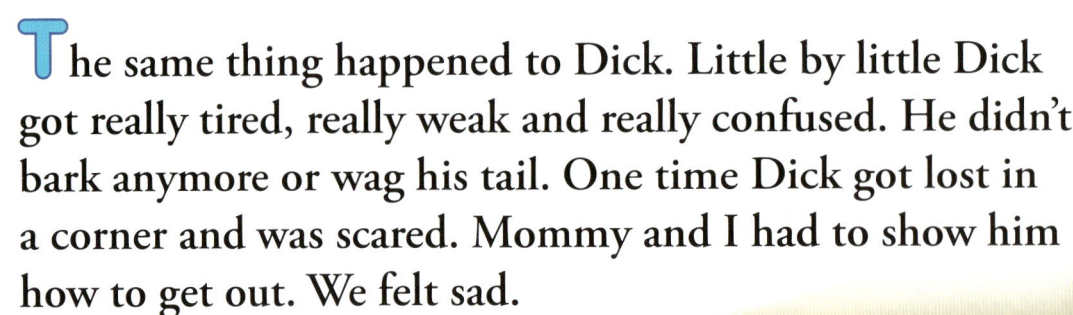

The same thing happened to Dick. Little by little Dick got really tired, really weak and really confused. He didn't bark anymore or wag his tail. One time Dick got lost in a corner and was scared. Mommy and I had to show him how to get out. We felt sad.

The doctor said it was this thing called dementia like our grandma had. Dick wasn't enjoying swimming, playing ball or even getting tummy rubs, anymore. I got all the treats but they didn't taste very good.

# SAYING GOODBYE

I didn't want to say goodbye to Dick, but Mommy said it was time. She said there is a rainbow bridge that he would cross. She said when he gets to the other side he would be able to romp and play with Grandma and with other dogs who walked across the rainbow bridge before him.

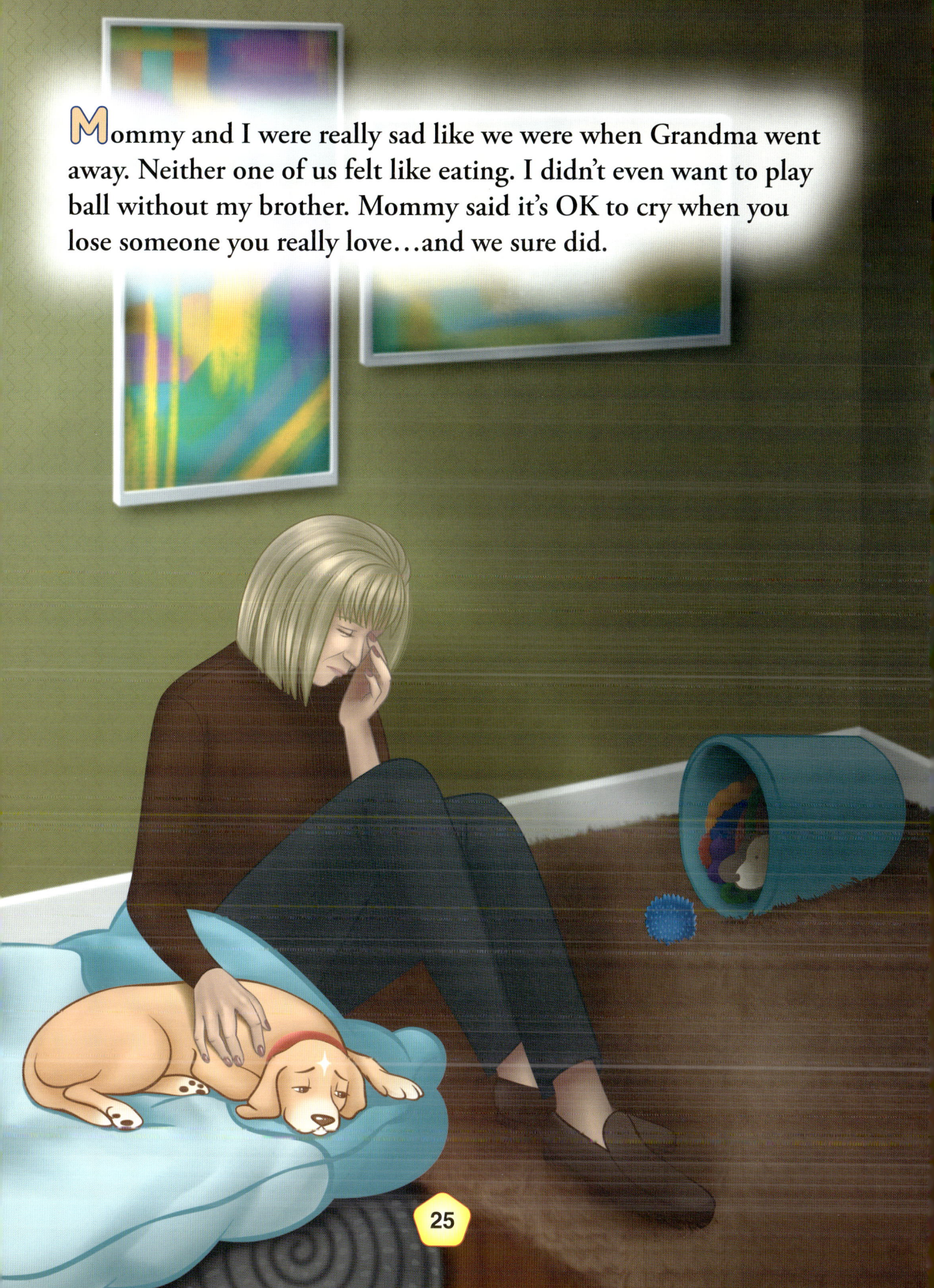

**M**ommy and I were really sad like we were when Grandma went away. Neither one of us felt like eating. I didn't even want to play ball without my brother. Mommy said it's OK to cry when you lose someone you really love…and we sure did.

Mommy's clients and friends had tears dripping from their eyes, too. Mommy got lots of cards, flowers and gifts. I got special hugs and tummy rubs...and even some treats and a toy.

# Christmas

Christmas came two months after Mommy and I said goodbye to Dick. Mommy decorated the house just like she always did. She still put up a stocking for Dick.

The Christmas tree was extra special that year. It had pretty lights and special ornaments. One ornament was an angel that said "Grandma." Another ornament was a paw print that said "Dick." There were ornaments for Mommy and me, too.

One day when Mommy and I came home from work, the Christmas tree skirt was all rumpled up. It happened three days in a row. On the third day, I finally sniffed the rumpled skirt. It smelled just like Dick. I plopped down on it—it felt all warm and cuddly. I fell asleep. It was then that I knew Dick was still with us.

# ONE YEAR LATER

Eventually my legs got tired and weak. I couldn't run and play and romp anymore. I still missed playing ball and getting into mischief with my brother.

Mommy said one day I would cross the rainbow bridge, too. I don't want to leave Mommy. She will cry so many tears without me, but I know Dick will be waiting for me with our magic ball in his mouth.

# Healing

We taught Mommy a lot of important things. Mostly, she learned to love, laugh, and live life to the fullest. The hard part was to let go when it was time. Mommy and we will always be happy we were a family. The love and memories will last forever.

Laugh

Love

Live life to the fullest

# Mommy's Favorite Pictures

Christmas 2019

Glasses

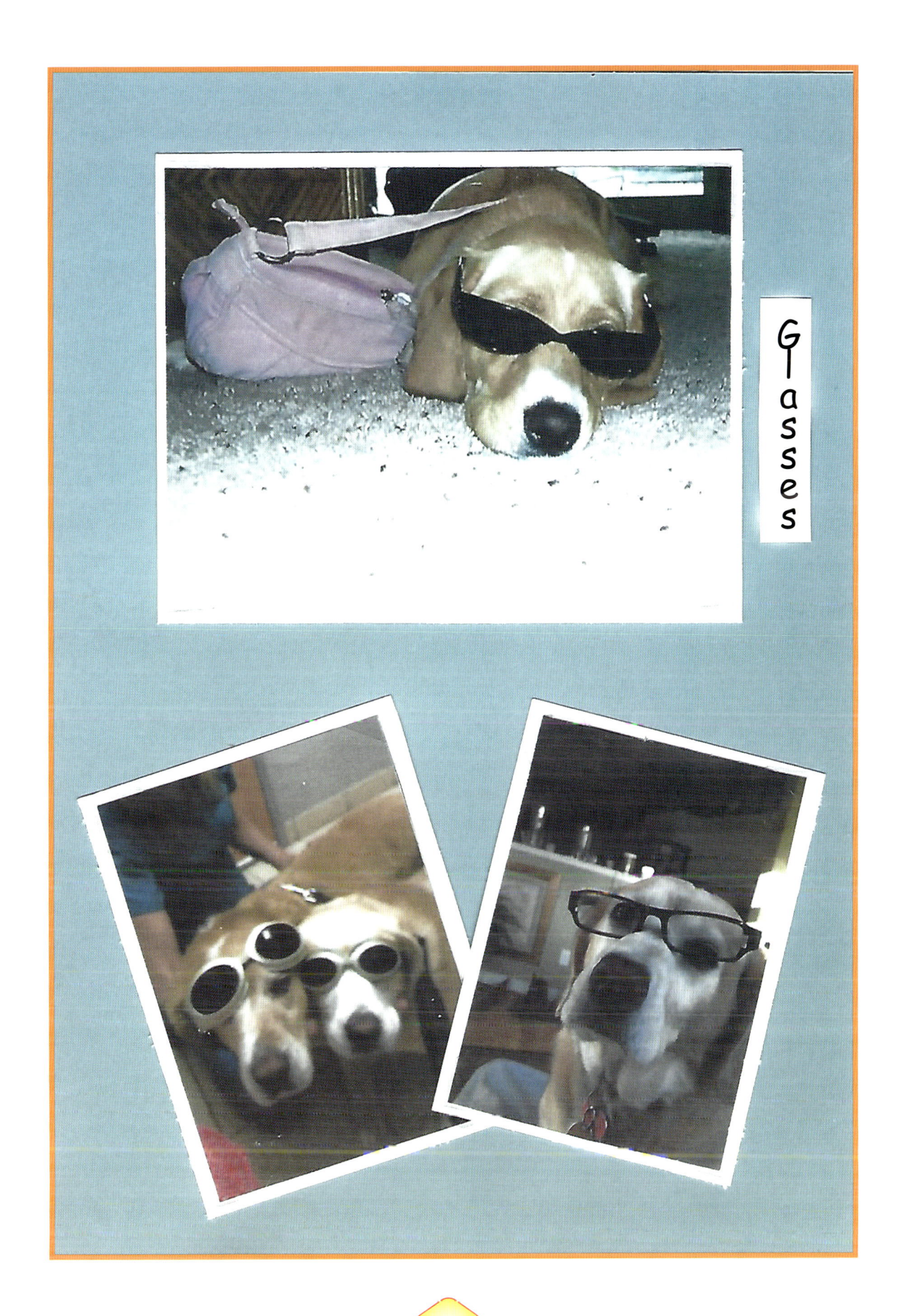

Mommy's Car

Cleaning

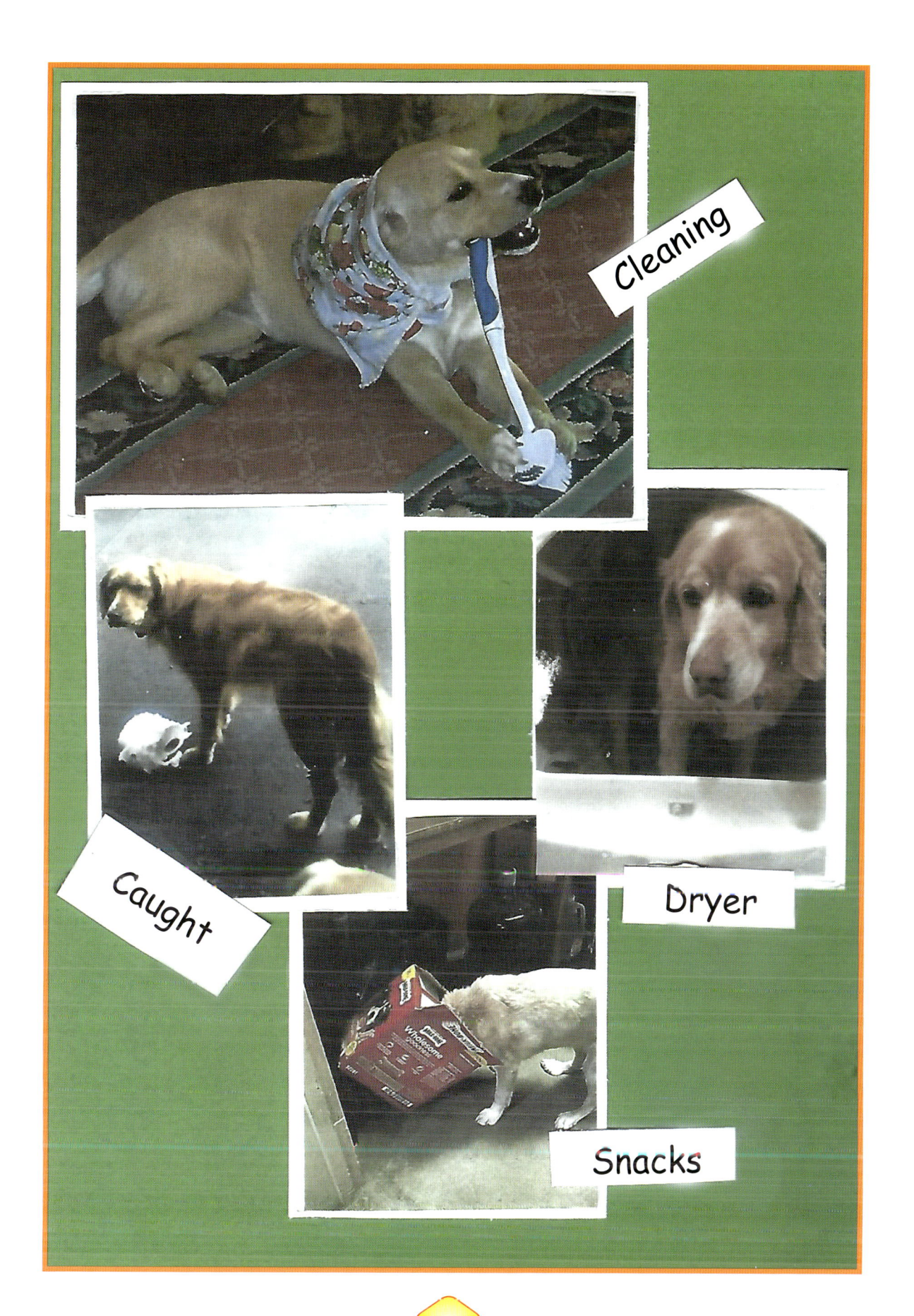

Caught

Dryer

Snacks

Cuddle

Buddies

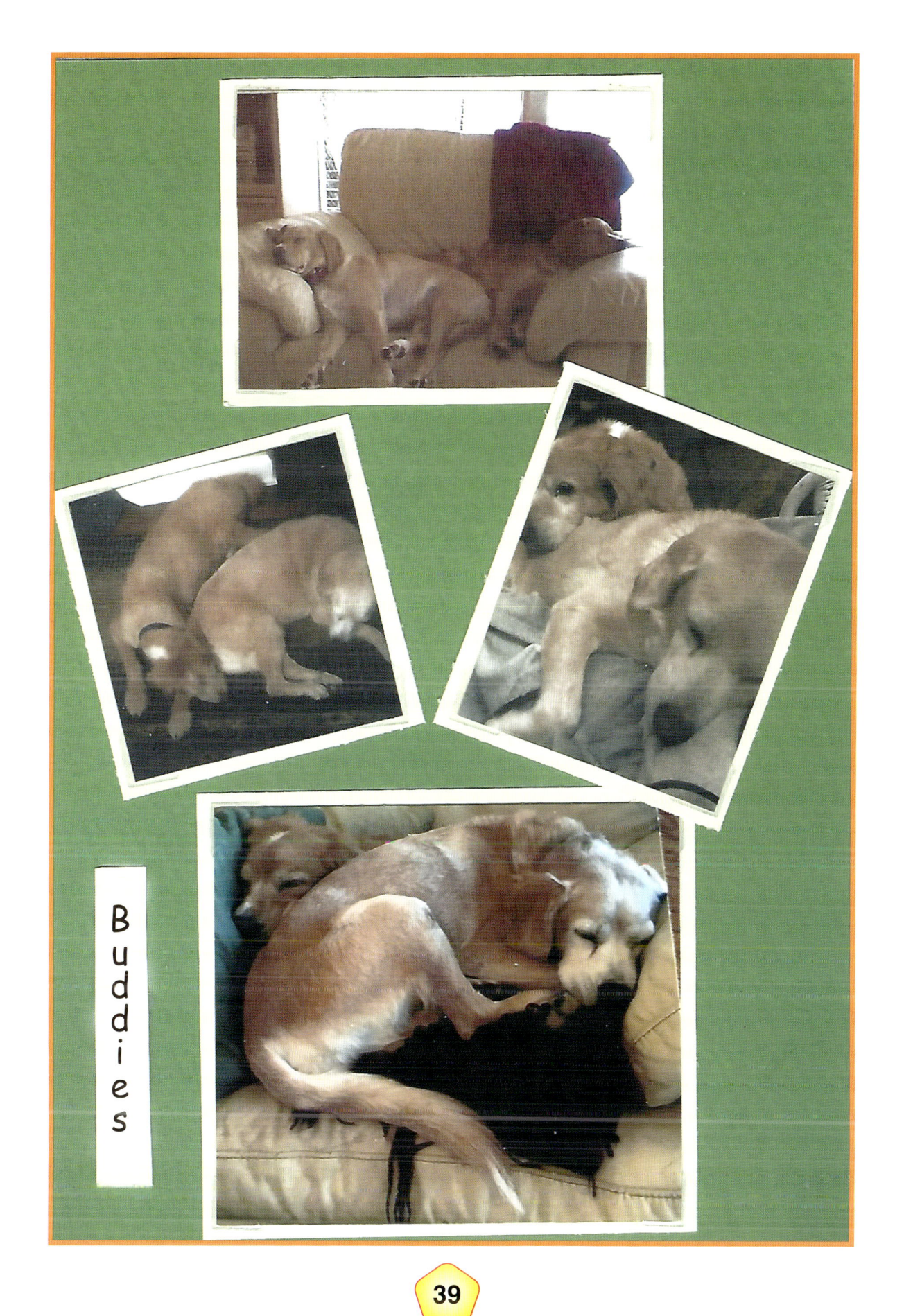

Snoozing

Do Not Disturb

May 7, 2021

Dick was here

Jane looking at photos of Dick and her before crossing the rainbow bridge

Hiding

Lost

Mommy's favorite pictures

Last Hugs

Forever Together

45

# Rainbow Bridge
adaptation by author

I remember our last moment right before we said goodbye
I looked at you and you looked at me while tears filled our eyes

I know it's hard to understand and I would have loved to stay
Somehow I knew I couldn't...I had to go away

So I will wait at the Rainbow Bridge until we meet again
And then it's balls, it's licks and tail wags for you
The best of all my friends

Never absent from our hearts

**Roseann** is a counseling psychologist who works in a small group practice in Elkhart, Indiana. This is the third book she has written and makes up the Dick and Jane series. It follows *Precious Moments with Dick and Jane* and *Double Trouble with Dick and Jane*. The books were inspired after many comments were made by clients who loved the real Dick and Jane and have benefited from their presence. Roseann has two children and four grandchildren who witnessed the antics of Dick and Jane. All of them provide love and laughter on a daily basis.

**Elena** has a passion for illustrating picture books for children. Her illustrations capture the eyes of children and adults alike. Elena uses her gift of art in designing business cards, postcards, posters, banners, and other creative products. She incorporates art in her free time in the form of chalk painting and CG illustrations.

Look for all three books in the Dick and Jane series.

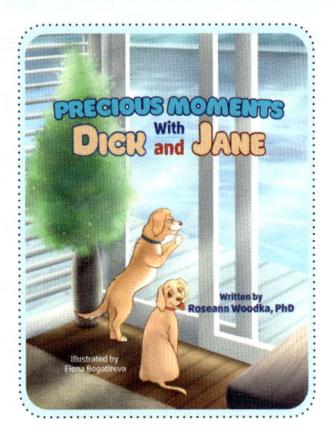

*Precious Moments with Dick and Jane.*

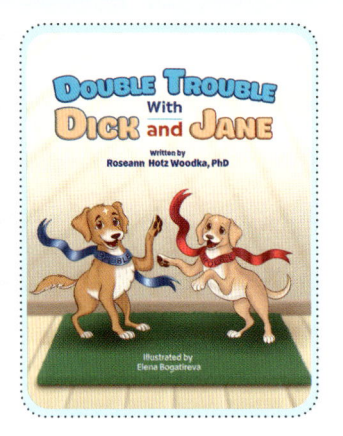

*Double Trouble with Dick and Jane*

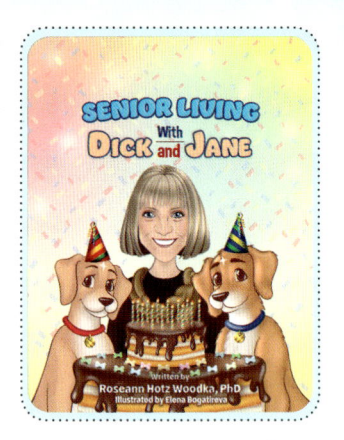

*Senior Living with Dick and Jane*

Thank you to Roger Carlson for patiently and diligently coordinating the Dick and Jane series: *Precious Moments with Dick and Jane*, *Double Trouble with Dick and Jane* and *Senior Living with Dick and Jane*. There is absolutely no way these books would have become a reality without you, Roger.

A special thank you to Brigitte Evens whose eye for creating photo pages added a personal touch to *Double Trouble with Dick and Jane* and *Senior Living with Dick and Jane*.

An additional thank you to Jenny Cooper, ("nice lady" who rescued Dick and Jane), my clients, friends, family, and co-workers who encouraged me as I wrote the Dick and Jane Series and who supported me when I had to say Goodbye to my fur babies.

*Find us on:*

@marianapublishing   @marianapublishing   @LlcMariana   Mariana Publishing Online

Copyright © 2021 by Mariana Publishing LLC

All rights reserved, including the right of reproduction in whole or in part in any form. This book or any portion thereof may not be reproduced or used in any manner whatsoever without the express written permission of the publisher except for the use of brief excerpts for review purposes.

ISBN: 978-1-64510-084-3 (IngramSpark Hardback)
ISBN: 978-1-64510-082-9 (Amazon Paperback)
ISBN: 978-1-64510-083-6 (POD)
ISBN: 978-1-64510-085-0 (POD Hardback)